A STEP-BY-STEP
SUCCESSFUL S

GW00537280

YOUR MILLION DOLLAR MESSAGE

How To Be A Highly Paid Speaker, Trainer or Consultant

Cydney O'Sullivan
12 Times Best Selling Author

Best Seller Success Publishing
Sydney, Australia
Australia Phone (61) 2 8005 4878
Las Vegas, Nevada, USA
US Phone 1 (702) 997 2229

Table of Contents

YOUR MILLION DOLLAR MESSAGE

How To Be a Highly Paid Speaker, Trainer or Consultant

So you'd like to be a highly paid speaker, trainer or consultant. Congratulations!

I'm excited to share with you what's been working for me and so many of my clients who are making hundreds of thousands to millions from speaking at events and running their workshops and offering training solutions.

I'm going to share with you how to use your knowledge and life experience for positioning so that your ideal clients start seeking YOU out, and FINDING you. **I'm going to show you how:**

- to brand yourself,
- to get more clients,
- to make more money,
- to get celebrity status if you want it,
- live a life of freedom,
- of joy

and have way, way, way more fun in your business.

Once you've read this book you'll understand the basics to creating a fortune in your speaking business. It's really quite a simple formula, but it does take a focused effort and a team to do this well. This report will tell you how to build your sales and marketing systems so that you can automate the process of finding new clients who are already keen to learn more from you, and how to help them feel comfortable to buy your products, packages and services and how to automate it all as much as possible.

I'm going to blast through the success formula that I've been teaching my paying clients to get clarity, and what I've seen work over and over in a variety of industries. I'm not going to hold back - I'm going to share what's helped us generate millions of dollars in new sales over the last 4 years, in the middle of the global recession.

Why Write This Book?

Have you ever felt depressed, frustrated and have no idea where to go or what to do next?

That's exactly where I was five years ago, after spending years building up my businesses and then having a major upheaval in my life. I felt completely overwhelmed and powerless, until I figured out the simple secrets to success in business today that has helped my clients and I create wealth much more easily and in a more sustainable way and I'm going to share that with you.

What I've learned over almost 30 years in business and mentoring other business owners and Startups is to know where to focus your attention for results.

As an experienced author, publisher and business coach I thought the secret to creating wealth on demand was to have great sales skills, and focused on using books to help my clients rise above their competition, I became a publishing consultant and 12 times bestselling author. I found that success could be achieved quickly but did NOT come from publishing the book.

What do I mean by that? Would you agree that writing a professional book full of great advice that showcases you as an expert in your field will help establish you as a more credible and authoritative choice over your competition who hasn't?

Do you know that writing such a book also gives you fantastic clarity about your expertise and how to share it with others? Did you know that when you back such a book up with a great website, strong social and traditional media engagement, and public speaking that it's an absolutely winning combination for success? Well, I can tell you that I have seen many experts use this combination to make hundreds of thousands to even millions of dollars.

Think about it - given no other introduction to an expert who are you more likely to perceive to be a credible expert - the fitness trainer who wrote a book on health, or the one who didn't? The Financial Adviser who wrote the book on wealth management, or the one who didn't?

> **To give you an example of how this works**, I work with many experts who use their author status to be engaged to speak to large crowds. While speaking they invite the audience to sign up or text in for a free guide or copy of their presentation. So every time they speak they add another large group of clients to their mailing list who have seen them at their most authoritative... **As the speaker, as a qualified expert**.
>
> Those with a great system in place can then invite all the people on their mailing list to attend trainings, or live events, or or simply send them special offers. This is a basic example of a marketing funnel.

The concept of a marketing or sales funnel is one of the most important aspects of the Speaking Stars Success™ formula, and one of the areas I see most commonly poorly executed by the businesses who come to me for help.

The term funnel is used to describe a process wherein you collect mass market interest in your business, product or service and then take them through a qualifying and nurturing process that turns them into leads, prospects and customers. Then, depending on the quality of your funnel and solutions, you want as many as possible to go on to become high value clients, repeat customers and refer you to other clients. If you do this really well they can even become raving fans!

Customer Lifetime Value

With this in mind you can work out what's called an average "Customer Lifetime Value" which is very helpful in determining who are your most profitable clients. To work this out you estimate how much does the average customer spend with you per purchase? How many times a year would they purchase? And how many years would they continue to purchase from you? Initially you'll estimate the LTV, but in time you should have a pretty accurate idea of the lifetime value of your customers.

Now, what I have learned from working with some of the most successful businesses in the world, and then working with hundreds of up and coming business owners was that there are some fundamentals that will make or break you in the new economy. So here's what successful businesses have in common:

I call it the Four Pillars of a strong business foundation.

The Formula to Speaking Stars Success – The Four P's

The formula is made up of 4 components and it's important to get them in the right order. Implementing them in the wrong order often leads to a massive waste of time, effort and lots of money.

They are:

1. **Positioning**
2. **Packaging**
3. **Promotion**
4. **Processes**

Once you know how to fill an event with the right audience, make an attractive offer that is of genuine value to some of the people in the audience and process your orders efficiently, then deliver on your sales promises, you can literally earn tens of thousands to millions of dollars per event.

If you don't want to run your own events, but become an accomplished speaker who is able to create a demand and close sales, you can make an equally impressive fortune speaking at other people's events, seminars, webinars, teleseminars, certification programs, and trainings. That's just a few of the places that you can find opportunities to practice sales presentations.

Building a seriously profitable speaking business takes commitment and considerable investment in yourself and your future. It takes time to trial, tweak and adjust your presentations to get them right, it takes practice and flexibility to be willing to work really diligently on a project and not always get it right for the audience. It takes the courage and resilience to keep at it until it pays off. But if you can do that, you can have a wonderful lifestyle, freedom and fun!

You can build a professional speaking business on your own, on the cheap if you are a talented designer, event organizer or experienced marketer, but seriously, when will you work on your speaking and all the other important aspects of your business? You don't need to do everything yourself. You can hire people who can help position you like the next Tony Robbins if you know where to find them.

There is a huge opportunity for experienced speakers now who just need to learn how to sell better and I want to help out as many honest, sincere people to do well in the speaking and training industry as I can.

The Foundational Pillars of The Speaking Stars Success Formula

Positioning

In the speaking and training business positioning yourself for success is an absolute game changer. In order to earn your place as a leader and the person in front of an audience, the key is to have a few fundamentals in place that help establish you as credible and authoritative. This will help you get the bookings, and fill your events.

1. To position yourself effectively as a leader in your area of expertise you should research your market and take the time to know your customer's needs, pains and pleasure points.

2. Understand the importance of and make the investment in developing a professional brand, bio and marketing message. This is where books and book series can be very helpful.

3. Seek out and invest in relationships with influencers and your marketplace and create alliances to faster leverage your credibility and open doors.

Packaging

**Once you are clear on your positioning, THAT is when
successful businesses develop Packaging**

1. Craft and practice your unique script to engage audiences
    and separate yourself from the competition

2. Create offers and products specifically tailored to your ideal
    market, they should feel highly valuable, irresistible and
    desirable.

3. Invest in marketing funnels that lead your audiences to
    offers that are relevant

Promotions

I see so many businesses pouring money into paid promotions
when they don't even have their positioning and marketing funnels
in place. This can drain your finances, distract your focus and
ultimately hurt your business.

1. Set up authoritative web presences to collect prospect
    contact information so you can build relationships and
    referral communities

2. Use marketing and media to get access to major
    distribution networks

3. Use cutting edge technologies like social media marketing,
    video marketing, and webcasts for greater reach and
    competitive edge.

All the while developing your automated systems...

Processes

This is an area I rarely see businesses getting right.

1. Successful businesses have simple systems that control the client experience from the first sales contact through to a paid product or service and even the after-sales experiences

2. Have simple sales processes that make it easy to take prospects to clients

3. Maximize the results of their marketing efforts and collect the revenues in the most automated and leveraged way possible, always reviewing and improving on their systems and customer experience.

Thanks to modern technologies even very small businesses can have professional processes now that allow them to process large orders and lots of sales. It's not unusual for well-organized speakers today to process hundreds of thousands of dollars in orders at a single event. They can take the annual revenue of most small to medium sized businesses in a few hours!

1. Choose Your Leadership Position

Choose your niche and topic of expertise

Your qualifications, life experience or passionate interests will largely determine what particular niche you choose to plant your stake in and call your own. But, if you're smart, you'll also take into consideration market demand, how 'cashed up' a market sector is and the competition.

Also research your local market and global market to find out who you are competing with in that category.

So how do you choose your niche? Here are some questions you can ask yourself that will help.

- Who are you?
- What have you done?
- What experience do you have that qualifies you?
- What is your life story?
- What formal qualifications do you have? (Not important if you don't have any of these, but if you do, might as well put them in the equation)
- How are you able to serve others?
- What solution could you provide and love doing it?
- What problem is not being solved that you would you like to solve? (You might identify more than one – in this case – answer the following for each of them)
- Who would your ideal clients be?
- How much would your ideal clients be prepared to pay for those solutions?
- How would you market those solutions to those ideal clients?
- How hard would that be for you to do?
- How long would it take you to set up?

Clarity of your message, how you're different from the others (USP)

Once you have an idea of what topic you'd like to speak about, it's time to focus on the clarity of your message and how your presentation will be special to you and different from others who are in your area of expertise.

Make a list of how you're similar to others who are teaching what you teach, and how you're different.

Many people find it useful to work out their USP or Unique Selling
Proposition. The job of your USP is to position your brand and
your offerings as the obvious and stand out choice to a purchaser
or booking agent because it makes it very clear how you're different
and better. Share your biggest point of difference that is of benefit to
your target market.

Keep it Simple!!

**Don't overcomplicate this process. This is where I see
most inexperienced people wasting effort, time and
money – making things much more complicated than
they need to be.**

**If you need help with clarity and your plan, book in for a
strategy call, at www.bestsellersuccess.com**

Claim Your Leadership Title

It really helps your target market to be able to say you're the leader
in your topic, even if it's as specific as "Australia's Leading Speaker
on Government Compliance Documentation" or "The No. 1 Leading
Trainer For Beauty Spa Staffing and Marketing"

Here are some questions to help you find your 'title:'

- What can you be the world's best at / leader of? Or...
- What could you be the nation's best at / leader of? Or...
- What could you be the local best at / leader of?
- Is there another person doing a great job with their
  positioning you could model? Who do you think their target
  market is and how are they talking the language of that
  customer base?

2. Create A Game Plan

At this stage you need a game plan that shows you understand your market, you've worked out the numbers, worked out the best marketing strategies, and delivery options so you can know when you'll hit your revenue targets. If you don't hit your targets, you'll be able to adjust the plan and know where you went wrong and correct the plan. Then you can leverage your sales and marketing funnels to allow you growth.

Here are some questions to help you set up your Game Plan:

- What is your five year goal – the big picture?

- What can you realistically set as one year goals? Consider earnings, costings and what team, mentoring, or support you'll need.

- A great way to set your goals is to reverse engineer them. For instance if you know you want to earn $100,000 in the next 12 months, and you feel comfortable that you can sell a $100 training, you can work out that over the course of the year you'll need to sell 1000 of these trainings. Then by dividing that number by 12 months you'll know how many you need to sell per month, which is about 84 trainings. If you feel comfortable you could sell 10 per speaking event, you'll need to speak about 8 times per month.

- How much time can you give it?

- How much can you invest?

- Who do you need on your team?

- Do you know enough to work out a step-by-step plan to roll out your launch and campaigns?
- If not, who can help you?

Shortcuts

Once you're executing your plan, there are plenty of shortcuts – outsourcing, modeling, and technology. These are advanced topics and I could write a book on each of these! Don't let these be distractions and delay your forward momentum.

> If you hire others to help where you are inexperienced or to manage areas that are not your strength it should pay off in speed to market. But be careful, finding genuine support in this industry is a bit of a minefield. Check out any service providers and support teams extensively. Do your due diligence.

If you really need shortcuts and want to discuss technology and outsourcing and your game plan you can book in for a strategy session with our team, or join one of our frequent webcast trainings or live events.

Build In Accountability All Along The Way

Expect life to get in the way for you and everyone working on your project.

- Set goals for yourself and monitor them. Put them on a calendar and check regularly to make sure you are on schedule. The people attracted to speaking as a career are often creative, social or perfectionists by their nature and can easily find themselves burned out after too many detours from the game plan.
- Set milestones for others in your support team and monitor them!

3. Write The Presentation To Get Clear On The Message

Now it's time to write your presentation. Here is what I advise most strongly:

- Create Your Presentation
- Test it to small audiences(webinar or small group of friends) before going live, practice, tweak and present again
- Test present again to a small, friendly live audience and incorporate valid and qualified feedback
- Test your presentation on another audience and incorporate valid and qualified feedback
- Practice, practice, practice

> If you need help crafting your presentation we do offer support in this area and because it's such a unique process for each individual we offer this as one of our services. We have a variety of processes to help you craft a professional and effective presentation in a way that is fast and simple for you.
>
> To find out more, please contact us at Support@MillionairesAcademy.com

What Makes a Good Speech – Crafting the Presentation

There are as many ways to give a speech as there are topics, audiences, and different kinds of people in the world. There are inspirational speeches, entertaining presentations, keynotes, educational and sales presentations to name just a few of the different styles.

For the purposes of this booklet I have focused on a combination of styles that is designed to engage the interest of the audience, invoke an emotional connection and create a desire in as many as possible that leads to them deciding to move forward with you in some way towards a commercial outcome.

Your speech should be entertaining, engaging, inspiring, authentic and paced so that your audience come on a journey with you. There are a number of well established techniques that you can incorporate into your presentation that encourage your audience to interact with, and feel more connected and trusting towards you. These can be learned in our advanced trainings, and they are very powerful.

Making Keynote Presentations and Trainings Profitable

Keynote speaking opportunities require very professional speaking standards, and are in high demand as there are a diminishing number of keynote speaking opportunities and an increasing amount of public speakers.

We encourage our clients to learn how to create demand and desire for their programs, coaching, consultancies or services and set those offers up so they are easy for people to buy, and then they can make almost any speaking opportunity profitable.

4. Establishing Your Expertise

Once you have your presentation and are clear on the area of expertise where you are going out to market, it's time to start building up your expert credibility.

Here are some ways to get started:

- **Social proof** – any awards, special achievements, client endorsements, well-known companies you've worked for or with, big name clients who don't mind you using their names on your websites and brochures

- **Case studies** – showcase your successes and those of your clients

- **Testimonials** – ask high profile people you've worked with to give you an endorsement or testimonial in writing, audio or video form. If you have audio or video it's easy to transcribe to written. Also get testimonials from your clients and customers. Think creatively, for instance even your suppliers might like to give you testimonials.

- **Media and Published Credibility** – if you've had any books published, articles, been featured in the newspaper, on the radio or on TV, consider adding these to your website and marketing.

- **Speaking Engagements** – if you've spoken with other big name speakers, or if you've spoken at big events. These can also be mentioned in your marketing collateral.

  If you need help with your websites and branding we do offer support in this area. We have been marketing best selling authors for many years so have a professional team to create branding, websites, media kits, book covers, and so on for most budgets. To find out more, please contact us at Support@MillionairesAcademy.com

Marketing Online

Marketing online has become one of the most cost-effective and results-effective ways to launch a business quickly and profitably in today's market.

I recommend:

- Register your name as a domain, eg. JackSmith.com and build an authority site that professionally showcases you, your area of expertise, your books and programs. This is a great place to show off all your credibility collateral as mentioned above and also to let people know how to contact you. This site should be search engine optimized to your name and your topics of expertise so that it ranks well when someone searches on those words.

- Build a professional business site that showcases your business and speaking programs that is search engine optimized to the terms people would use to find you as a solution provider or speaker in your niche.

- Have a professional LinkedIn profile as this social media is very search engine optimized and is often a source professionals will use to check you out. It's also worth investing some time to connect here with other professionals in your industry and expand your circle of influence

- Other social media platforms: at very least claim your name and business name as business pages on Facebook, Twitter and Pinterest.

Don't Be Cheap on Your Way to Success!

Remember! Don't be cheap on your branding and websites

Professionals want to work with other professionals and they WILL check you out and they will judge you on ugly, outdated, or cheap looking websites and marketing materials. Invest in your professional image.

If you need help with your social media and online marketing we do offer support in these areas. We have been marketing speakers and best selling authors for many years so have a professional team to create Facebook business pages, advertising campaigns, social media engagement and LinkedIn, Twitter and Pinterest for most budgets.

5. Packages

What should you sell as a professional speaker?

Firstly, make sure you like doing what you're selling and want to talk about it and help people on an ongoing basis. For instance, one of the problems with the self-improvement market is the amount of people you'll be working with who are down and out. This can be very emotionally draining when you are supporting these people on a long-term and ongoing basis.

I have worked with a lot of clients who were weight loss experts who are now just sick of dealing with the same issues over and over again after years in the business.

Other People's Products and Services, Training, or Programs

Where most people first get into giving public presentations is either as an educator or trainor or selling for others as part of their job, or often people find out they are a good speaker while promoting network marketing programs.

Selling other people's products is a great place to start. I started out selling other people's programs and it worked out really well for me. I have sold the programs of hundreds of big speakers and that is how I know so much about the industry now.

> If you need help creating your books and programs we do offer support in these areas. We have been creating our own training programs and assisting speakers and best selling authors to create theirs for many years so have a professional team to create membership sites, telesummits, webinarsummits, and CD or DVD set trainings for most budgets. Please contact us at Support@MillionairesAcademy.com

You Might Prefer to Sell Your Own Programs, Coaching and Trainings

I recommend that once you know your niche and topic you write books about it and that will give you the foundations to create training programs, coaching programs, certification trainings and programs. Or you might prefer to create your consulting, coaching or training program and produce books later, or never at all.

Tips:

- Create your packages in a way that makes it very easy for people to buy

- Make them relevant, market appropriate and competitive

6. Marketing Funnels – The Magic Formula to Acquire and Nurture leads

I touched on Marketing Funnels earlier in this report, and these are magic once effectively planned, built and set in place. This is one of the most important aspects of the success formula, and one of the areas I see most commonly left out, botched up or poorly executed. Not setting up marketing funnels is literally leaving most of the cash in your business completely and inexcusably untapped.

The term funnel is used to describe a process wherein you promote a mass market offer that should engage the interest of your target market audience to your business, product or service and then take them through a qualifying and nurturing process.

The goal of the nurturing process is to convert the leads who show initial interest into leads, then through a natural filtering process, convert some of them into customers, depending on the quality of your funnel and solutions.

Your goal from the funnel is for as many as possible to go on to become high value clients, repeat customers who purchase other products and services or yours over and over, and refer you to other clients. If you do this really well they can even become raving fans!

Because everyone's niche and offering will vary, it's best I just give a brief explanation of how to set up a funnel. It's quite a strategic process.

- Promote an entertaining or educational introductory offer
- Enlist leads to trust you with their contact information
- Follow up with enticing and relevant offers
- Continue to provide entertaining or high value educational content to build further trust and recognition of your brand
- Continue to provide valuable and engaging offers
- Use technology and automation wherever possible

You'll also need good marketing copy, well written emails, and social media posts, should you decide to also use that as a promotional tool. Marketing funnels can also be built straight from social media platforms such as Facebook, allowing you to set up marketing campaigns without requiring websites.

These are advanced marketing strategies. Start with as simple a marketing funnel as possible and we are happy to help when you are ready for more complex strategic implementation and guidance.

If you need help creating your marketing funnels we offer support in this area. We have been creating our own training programs and assisting speakers and best selling authors to create theirs for many years so have a professional team to create complex launch and marketing campaign funnels and automated marketing and promotion systems.

To find out more, please contact us at Support@MillionairesAcademy.com

7. Set Up Your Delivery Process and Systems

Make sure whatever you sell – you can deliver!

You need to be able to deliver what market. Few things will hurt your business more than getting your positioning right, your packaging right, your sales working and then failing to deliver on your promise.

It's much harder to win a customer back after a bad experience than to get them to try something new. Remember that a happy customer will tell a few of their friends about it, but an unhappy customer will tell just about everyone who will listen about it – and today the reach of an unhappy customer is greater than ever thanks to review sites, social media and other technologies of mass communications.

Automation and technology

I recommend products and services that can be delivered digitally with all of today's modern technologies. Though with the amazing online retail facilities that are available, it's not hard to deliver books and programs through Amazon, eBay and other similar online platforms that have massive audiences and distribution networks in place already.

8. Promotion

Effective Marketing

In today's market you can spend money in so many ways when it comes to promotion: Print ads, letterbox drops, direct mail, telemarketing, Pay Per Click (eg. Google, Linkedin or Facebook advertising), Public Relations (PR), classifieds, radio, solo ads, pay per view, infomercials, social media marketing, and video marketing…. It's very confusing. I've seen what works because so many of our clients have tried so many types of promotions.

I recommend you focus on marketing that monetizes along the way. Whether it's starting with free marketing options and seeing what works, or paid advertising – there will be some mediums and strategies that are more effective than others, depending on your topic, niche, offer and target markets.

I regularly assist clients who have been paying thousands of dollars a month on advertising that is not bringing in enough business to even pay for the advertising. Our first goal is to get them out of these situations as quickly as possible and get that revenue working much more effectively for them.

Getting your marketing right can make the difference between getting in front of 5 people a month and 5000 people a month, and making lots of sales or pouring money down the drain with a fire hose sized tap. With today's technologies **our clients regularly make $50,000 to a $100,000 dollars** from a simple, but strategic, marketing campaign.

If your marketing is not producing **revenue**, it's almost certainly the wrong marketing.

If you'd like some help we are a team of experienced results-focused professionals.

Simply contact us at Support@MillionairesAcademy.com

When you are starting out there are a few promotional strategies I recommend that will be helping you build your business and are very cost effective.

Public Speaking

If done right, public speaking is quite simply one of the most cost and time effective strategies to promote your business and promote your services. It's pure gold.

You can add hundreds of new prospects to your mailing list who have seen you speak as an authority, know what your message is, and be far more connected and warmly engaged with you than through any other medium.

Webinars & Teleseminars

Webcasts and telecasts also known as webinars and teleseminars are a brilliant and now easily accessible technology to do trainings and speeches from online to an audience anywhere in the world. I have done webinars with attendees from all over the world at once! Depending on the platform you choose, you can accommodate an audience of 1 to thousands. And the cost per broadcast will most likely vary by such factors as number of attendees, though there are now plenty of free options for broadcasting over the internet.

We, and our clients, have made tens of thousands of dollars from webinar and teleseminar presentations, and they are very simple to run and very cost effective. They are also brilliant for creating training programs and recording client consulting or coaching sessions.

Social Media

Most people have social media accounts now, such as Facebook and LinkedIn so a great place to start building up a supportive community for your events, speaking engagements and campaigns is by connecting with social media.

Social media promotional campaigns can be very effective, but do take some time to set up properly and we recommend that this tends to be more of an advanced strategy unless you are a great networker and already have a large following of your target market to promote to.

Emails

Have an effective emailing system in place and crafting engaging emails should be part of your promotional strategy. Then focus on building up your subscriber list.

9. Sales

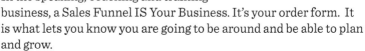

Sales Funnels

This is such an important element to your
marketing process. For most businesses
sales success is the revenue life force.
In the speaking, coaching and training
business, a Sales Funnel IS Your Business. It's your order form. It
is what lets you know you are going to be around and be able to plan
and grow.

It's how you utilise your Marketing Funnel to nurture a prospect and
cold lead into a warm lead so should your Sales Funnel nurture your
buyers into long term clients. Sales Funnels make you millions.
Packaging makes you hundreds of thousands. Sales Funnels create
buyers for life and create far greater profits. The packages are a part
of the funnel.

To give you a quick example using the image of a funnel as seen here;
the red area at the top might be where your prospects start spending
money. They may spend $1 to $100 - that's part of your pricing
strategy. The orange then takes them to a higher level spend, say
$500. As the funnel narrows, your buyers start to show consistent
buying habits and confidence in YOUR business.

When you ask them to spend more money, they have more trust and
experience with you and are more likely to do so. They have been
forming a relationship with you - even if they are not conscious of it.
The best part about a sales funnel is you can actually dollarize the
value of a lead and the value of a customer. This is a great tool to sort
out your Customer Life Time Value.

Scripts

I have found scripts to be fabulous because they can also be used to multiply the results of a great sales result in that they can be duplicated by other sales people.

So I am a big fan of scripts. So what is it that I mean when I say, you need a script? And what does that have to do with a sales funnel? Well if you are going to build an effective and efficient business, you are going to have processes. In this business the Sales Funnel is very much process #1. I hope by now you can see that I want you to think of each sale as not just a one-off purchase, but a life-long client relationship.

So scripts are to sales what Xero, MYOB or Quickbooks is to your Accounting department. You and your (sales) team create a flow, a consistency, a process through which you use your scripts to assist people through your funnel. You should have a questionnaire and guideline to follow that allows you to keep the conversations heading in the right direction.

Selling

If you think you can build up a successful speaking, training or coaching business and get out of doing any selling, think again. In my experience it's not enough to be a great speaker or consultant or trainer. The truth is that we are always selling. If you have ever been in a relationship or have children, you have had to learn to be a master of influence.

Influence is what closes the sale, and it's what helps our customers find us, trust us, and how we improve their lives. So we all use it on some level - we just have to get over all the baggage associated with the word 'sales' - or – on an even deeper level, the baggage associated with asking for money.

If you are not selling your services or products, then you are not serving the world with your true gifts. You are cheapening your brand and hurting the industry in which you should be a proud leader and specialist. If you aren't joyfully selling in your business, I'd like to help you get over whatever is holding you back - quickly and seriously. Because you are here reading this book about being ready to launch and if you don't get this one thing sorted, all the hard work you put in will come to a bottleneck and hold back your success!

Follow-up: *Do you want $1 million or will you stop at $100,000?*

Let's start with a story. There are different types of selling styles, and some salespeople are hunters while others are farmers. Although I'm not an expert in selling, I am very good with follow up. When you follow up properly, people feel connected to your team and your company because you care and stay in touch.

On the sales floor with a major promoter in Australia, I was closing $50,000 sales while the others in the sales team were having trouble closing $1,000 or $5,000 sales. The clients would even thank me for following up and checking on them and thank me for taking their $50,000, and continue to stay in touch for years.

The secret was in the follow up. Sometimes you will have clients who just really can't commit to buy right now. As much as you worry that they will spend their money to a greater salesperson who may not offer as good a service as you, you'll just have to believe them.

If you find yourself living in perpetual follow up, then you probably have a serious closing problem and aren't looping - in which case you need to talk to us. Sometimes people's indecision holds them back and in that case, there is a technique called "Looping" which can assist them very effectively to a happy close.

But following up is quite important and staying in touch with them can be automated using a well designed sales funnel. With the technology we have today, there is no reason that you cannot do this quite easily and it usually makes a huge financial impact on the business.

Our way of selling is very conscious of the client and the experience. It is about building a relationship and trusting one another, and then creating a community.

We do this with you in your business because it is what makes the millions - not just the smoke and mirrors that causes so many to ultimately crash and burn.

10. Where To From Here?

There are great emotional and financial rewards to those who succeed in this industry. Freedom, recognition, and the joy of being able to facilitate the ongoing transformation of yourself and others. Sharing your gifts for financial and spiritual wealth, and being able to help those less fortunate.

I know that doing all of this alone can be quite trying and difficult. Being an expert performer is hard enough, let alone running the show behind the scenes. And if you have been running your own business, workshops and events, you realise that filling up rooms is a job in and of itself, let alone having the time to give the best presentation.

Are you ready? 5 questions to ask yourself to find out if you're ready

1. Do I love this area of expertise?

2. Do I enjoy and get satisfaction and fulfillment from helping and serving people?

3. Can I see myself in 5 - 10 - 20 years continuing to provide support to people in
    this way?

4. Am I committed to making time to building this business?

5. What part of the **Speaking Stars Success™ 4 P** sequence am I currently at, and which of the 4 P's do I need help with?

Can we help you?

We love to help! It's why we're in business.

We also offer full service consulting and done-for-you support programs that cover:

- Website design and development
- Social media marketing
- Publishing
- Marketing funnels
- Sales scripts & copywriting
- Presentation Writing and Speaker Coaching

If you'd like some help with your marketing, we are a team of experienced results-focused professionals. Simply contact us at Support@MillionairesAcademy.com

Where you can meet us:

We are based in Sydney, Australia and Las Vegas, Nevada

We regularly hold live workshops in Sydney, and several times a year
hold workshops in Las Vegas and other US and Australian cities. To
join our community and find out about our workshops please visit
our website www.MillionairesAcademy.com

To Your Great and Fabulous Success!!

Cydney O'Sullivan

Cydney O'Sullivan is the founder of **MillionairesAcademy.com,**
a program that assists experts to turn their knowledge into wealth,
and share their wisdom with international audiences through the
power of public speaking and training programs.

**Contact us at www.MillionairesAcademy.com
or by emailing Support@MillionairesAcademy.com**

About the Author

Publishing and presentations consultant **Cydney O'Sullivan** shares her time between two teenagers, consulting, and travelling to international conferences. She is a Global Citizen of the world, splitting her time between Australia, Las Vegas, and Los Angeles. She has been investing in successful businesses from seed projects to IPOs for over 30 years.

Most of her career she has been a business 'turn around' expert. In her years as a business, real estate and stock market investor she has made millions. But, along with her success, she also made some costly mistakes; and this motivated her to rebuild her own wealth. In the process she became a caring mentor, assisting others toward their own success. She is a proud supporter of micro-economic lending and social business projects.

She has written and published several no. 1 best selling books; **Social Marketing Superstars**, Social Media Mystery to Mastery in 30 Days; **How to Be Wealthy NOW!** 108 Fast Cash Solutions; **Quantum Leap My Life**, and several other books based on her own experience of turning value and service into revenue.

Her business advice has been featured in national newspapers and magazines and in many books including: **The World's Greatest Speakers**, with Brian Tracy and Suze Orman, **Secrets of Inspiring Women Exposed!, Motivational Speakers America**, The Indispensable Guide to America's Business and Motivational Speakers, and multiple editions of **Motivational Speakers Australia**. She is the founder of several training programs including Experts Success, Rocket Your Sales, Millionaires Academy, Best Seller Success, Expert Success Summit and Social Superstar Secrets.

Cydney is also the founder and CEO of the top ranking speaker's agency **Motivational Speakers International**. Please visit www.MotivationalSpeakersInternational.com to book Cydney or other professional speakers and trainers for your events, retreats and conferences.

CPSIA information can be obtained
at www.ICGtesting.com
Printed in the USA
LVHW01s1004230218
567631LV00003B/4/P